EUROPA ⚔ MILITARIA Nº 2

CHALLENGER SQUADRON

Simon Dunstan

The Crowood Press

First published in 1999 by
The Crowood Press Ltd
Ramsbury, Marlborough, Wiltshire SN8 2HR

British Library Cataloguing-in-Publication Data
A catalogue record for this book is available
from the British Library

ISBN 1 86126 301 5

Edited by Martin Windrow
Designed by Tony Stocks/Compendium
Printed and bound by Craft Print, Singapore

Dedication:
To 'Sprocket' Spencer-Smith RTR,
a soldier of the old school
and a mechanical wizard, to whom
the tank remains a source of wonder.

Acknowledgements:
The author wishes to thank the following for their kind and generous
assistance in the preparation of this book:

The National Army Museum; Walter Böhm; Lt.Col.A.Groves RGR,
DPR(A); Dennis Lunt; Lt.Col.J-D von Merveldt RGJ, Chief of Press
Office BFG; Tim Neate; Public Information British Forces Germany;
Public Information Land Command Wilton; David Rowlands; Jenny
Spencer-Smith; The Tank Museum; Vickers Defence Systems;
and to the following Regiments of the Royal Armoured Corps for their
patience and forbearance in the face of my numerous enquiries about
BATUS, Bosnia, ballistics, Bovington, battlegroups, Baraci, bag
charges, *et al:* 1st The Queen's Dragoon Guards; The Royal Scots
Dragoon Guards; The Royal Dragoon Guards; The Queen's Royal
Hussars; The King's Royal Hussars; The Queen's Royal Lancers; 1st
Royal Tank Regiment; 2nd Royal Tank Regiment.

Unless otherwise stated, all photographs are courtesy of the Director of
Public Relations (Army) Ministry of Defence.

Front cover:
A Challenger 1 Mark 3 of 2 Troop, D Squadron, The Queen's Royal
Hussars, reverses out of a fire position during Exercise First Crusade on
Salisbury Plain, October 1996. (Simon Dunstan)

Back cover:
Challengers of 3 Troop, A Squadron, 14th/20th King's Hussars, during
final training before the land offensive to liberate Kuwait in February
1991.

Challenger Squadron

During the Second World War British tanks were consistently inferior to their German counterparts - only in the scale of production were the two countries comparable, with each manufacturing approximately 24,000 tanks between 1939 and 1945. However, as compared to earlier designs, the final British tank to emerge in the closing days of the war showed considerable promise. Forged in the crucible of war, Centurion was an admirable design with considerable growth potential. This was just as well, since in its original form it displayed no major advance over the German Panther introduced in 1943.

Based on bitter experience - in the wastes of the Western Desert, among the steep hills of Tunisia and Italy, in the blind maze of the dreaded Normandy *bocage*, on the exposed embankments of the Dutch *polders*, and in the dank twilight of the Reichswald - British designers vowed never again to allow British soldiers to enter battle with tanks of inferior firepower or armour protection to those of their potential foes.

The emergence of the formidable JS-3 Josef Stalin heavy tank at the Allied Forces Victory Parade in May 1945 did much to galvanise Western armies to seek a comparable design. In Britain this gave rise to the concept of the Capital Tank, later to emerge as the Main Battle Tank; but as an interim measure a heavy tank, Conqueror, was

(**Above**) A prototype FV4030/4 makes a dramatic entrance through a cloud of coloured smoke grenades in the first public demonstration to the press. The red triangle on the side of the turret denotes that it is not fitted with Chobham armour, or indeed any armour plate. Several such models were used for extensive mobility trials, and later for public display (where no amount of tapping or inspection could glean any knowledge as to the configuration of Chobham armour, which to this day remains a closely-guarded secret).

devised to support Centurion formations by engaging Soviet armour at long ranges. Either acting as the fourth tank in a Centurion troop (in the manner of the 17pdr. Sherman Firefly of 1944), or equipping the fourth troop in a squadron, Conqueror mounted a 120mm main gun and heavy armour protection. Its weight of 65 tons inevitably compromised mobility, both tactical and strategic.

Accordingly, a solution was sought which combined the heavy firepower of Conqueror with the mobility and reliability of Centurion. By the innovative use of a supine driving position and a radical turret configuration, the resulting design emerged as Chieftain, armed with a 120mm gun, which replaced both Conqueror and Centurion from 1967 and thus became the first Main Battle Tank to see service with the British Army.

However, the design was compromised (not to say cursed) by a NATO decision to install a multi-fuel engine

- one that was capable of running on aviation fuel, petrol, diesel or even domestic heating oil. Whereas other tank-producing NATO countries soon realised that such a powerplant was impractical and adopted conventional diesel engines, Britain persisted with an unsatisfactory design derived from a Junkers Jumo aero-engine which, when fitted inside a compact armoured envelope, proved chronically unreliable (even though it only ever ran on diesel fuel). It was to take almost 20 years to achieve a satisfactory level of performance, and even then the power-to-weight ratio for a tank of 55 tonnes was marginal, although Chieftain's firepower and armour protection were second to none.

It is customary that as soon as a tank enters service the design of its successor gets underway; and during the 1970s it was deemed desirable to undertake joint development programmes of major weapon systems, both to promote standardization within NATO and to defray procurement costs. However, national aspirations are profoundly difficult to reconcile; and so it proved in the Anglo-German Future Main Battle Tank programme to replace Chieftain and Leopard 1, which was eventually cancelled in 1977.

Britain then pursued a unilateral design known as MBT-80; but this incorporated several overly sophisticated technological innovations which proved impossible to

(Above) The FV4030 series was designed for the Imperial Iranian Army and originally designated Shir Iran ('Lion of Persia'); the final model emerged as Shir 2. After buying almost 800 Chieftains during the 1970s the Iranians had requested a tank of significantly greater engine power and reliability. Their oil revenues were to fund the FV4030 design and development cycle, until the fall of the Shah led to the cancellation of the contract for almost 1,200 vehicles at a cost of £1 billion. This view shows the main identifying differences between the Shir 2 and Challenger prototypes; the former has a Condor sight at the commander's cupola and external conduits leading to the smoke dischargers.

(Opposite above) With the collapse of the separate British Army programme to design a successor for both Chieftain and Leopard 1 in conjunction with Germany, and of the technologically over-ambitious MBT-80 programme, the Army was

obliged to adopt the FV4030 as an interim measure. This model still shows various aspects of Shir 2, such as the atmospheric crosswind sensor on a stalk at the turret rear, which was dispensed with on Challenger to save money.

(Right) An FV4030/4 prototype negotiates a knife-edge during mobility trials at Bovington by ATDU (Armoured Trials and Development Unit). The steering units incorporated in the TN37 transmission were so untrustworthy that prototypes had to be towed by a venerable turretless Conqueror from the main compound at the Military Vehicles & Engineering Establishment, Chertsey, Surrey, across the bridge over the M3 motorway to the test track - for fear that if the Challenger was driven under its own power the steering might fail in mid-passage and plunge the tank onto the busy carriageway below. On those occasions when the old Conqueror tug failed to start, trials of the FV4030 had to be suspended until it was repaired.

4

implement at a satisfactory price. With costs spiralling out of control, the programme was terminated - leaving the British Army with a fleet of ageing Chieftains at a time when the Soviet Union was introducing ever more effective MBTs by the thousand.

As an interim measure the British Army was obliged to adopt a version of an MBT designated FV4030, which was originally designed for the Imperial Iranian Army. With the fall of the Shah of Iran in 1979 the Khomeini regime cancelled the complete contract for 1,200 tanks, but not before the first 200 models of FV4030/3 or Shir 2 had been paid for and production was underway at Royal Ordnance Factory Barnbow in Leeds. This model featured Chobham armour, which represented a quantum leap for-

(Opposite) A view of the turret assembly line gives a good comparison between the conventional cast turrets of Chieftain (second from foreground), and the Chobham-armoured type of Challenger (foreground), which is fabricated. These Chieftain turrets are actually for the FV4030/2 or Khalid, as it was designated by the Royal Jordanian Army, which ordered 274 examples in November 1979 at a cost of £266 million.

ward in armour technology; it gave greatly enhanced protection against attack from all types of weapons but especially from chemical energy rounds.

With its coffers unexpectedly awash with Iranian petrodollars, and being presented with ever-increasing bills for the MBT-80 programme, the Treasury demanded the cancellation of the latter and the immediate procure-

(Right) Following an initial MOD order placed in September 1979 for 243 MBTs at a cost of £300 million, production of Challenger was undertaken at the Royal Ordnance Factory at Barnbow in Leeds. Here, the 1,200bhp powerpack is being fitted on the hull assembly line. Barnbow has been one the most important tank factories in Britain, producing AFVs since the Second World War. In July 1986 Vickers Defence Systems purchased the factory following the privatization of Royal Ordnance Factories; and in 1998 VDS announced that Barnbow was to close.

ment of the FV4030 by the MOD. This decision preclud-
ed any further development of the design, which was
known to be deficient in certain aspects - notably in the
fire control system, which was essentially identical to that
of current models of Chieftain. With distinct reservations
the General Staff accepted the new tank, now named
Challenger, into service in December 1982.

Challenger entered regimental service in April 1983,
completing troop trials with The Royal Hussars early the
following year. The new tank was first deployed on an
FTX (Field Training Exercise) on 16 September 1984
during Exercise Lionheart 84 near Hildesheim in West
Germany. (Interestingly, this was also the first time that
the M1 Abrams and the M2 Bradley were seen in the field
in Europe, while the MCV80 - later to enter service as
Warrior - also made its first appearance in prototype
form.)

For several years, however, Challenger was incapable
of fulfilling its true potential due to the severe financial
constraints imposed by the government. These curtailed
track mileages on exercises; the provision of spare parts;
the introduction of modern training aids; and the necessary improvements to keep Challenger abreast of its con-
temporaries and evolving technology. The result of such
parsimony was demonstrated to embarrassing effect during the Canadian Army Trophy of 1987, when Challenger
came last in the NATO tank gunnery competition by a
significant margin. Despite this debacle a mid-life
improvement programme for Challenger was not institut-
ed, and resources were devoted to the Chieftain replace-

ment programme which was becoming long overdue.

Such was the dissatisfaction with Challenger within
some circles of the British Army that there were demands
for the MOD to forgo any further delays and procure an
off-the-shelf design from abroad with immediate effect;
the *de facto* choice was a modified version of the M1A1
Abrams, as the British would never contemplate any tank
with a main armament of less that 120mm, while the
Leopard 2 was perceived as deficient in regard to armour
protection.

In the event a stringent competitive procurement exercise was undertaken between the contemporary US,
German (and later French) MBTs, as well as a new model
of Challenger being developed by Vickers Defence
Systems (VDS) which was designated Challenger 2,
while the original Challenger became Challenger 1. The
decision as to which MBT was to equip the British Army
was to be taken in December 1990; but, following the
invasion of Kuwait by the Iraqi regime of Saddam
Hussein in August 1990, this was deferred until the campaign to liberate Kuwait was over.

An important element of Operation Desert Sabre was
the force of 176 Challenger 1 MBTs of 1st (UK)
Armoured Division, which was assigned to the US 7th
Corps in the major offensive to outflank the Iraqi forces in
Kuwait and destroy the Republican Guard divisions held
in reserve. With a comprehensive up-armouring package
and a generous allocation of spares, Challenger 1 proved
to be highly effective in combat, destroying numerous
Iraqi tanks and AFVs without any losses to enemy action.

In consequence, Challenger 2 was chosen in June 1991 to replace Chieftain; and it was subsequently decided to procure a total of 386 of the new MBTs, which would supersede Challenger 1 as well. The first regiment to be equipped with Challenger 2 was The Royal Scots Dragoon Guards in June 1998, followed by 2nd Royal Tank Regiment; and by the end of the year 2000 all will be in service with six armoured regiments. Challenger 2 has considerable growth potential, as evidenced in the export model currently offered by VDS which incorporates a German 1,500 bhp MTU EuroPowerPack and further improvements to the fire control system under the designation Challenger 2E - 'E' for Enhanced. Other potential options include 140mm main armament; an automatic target acquisition and tracking system; various threat detection devices and countermeasures to thwart them; a supplementary up-armouring package of Explosive Reactive Armour arrays over the front and sides of the vehicle, as well as the increasingly important aspects of digital battlefield management systems.

It is probable that Challenger 2 will be the last Main Battle Tank to be produced by Britain on her own. Even now Challenger 2E draws over 50 per cent of its components from international sources. As the original inventor of the tank, Britain has a rich history in the design and manufacture of armoured fighting vehicles, and the Challenger is but one in a long line which first entered battle on the Somme in September 1916. Hopefully, Challenger will also prove to have been the last to go to war.

(Opposite) One of seven prototypes is put through its paces at the ATDU at Bovington. In an accelerated development programme between late 1980 and late 1982, more than 100,000km of automotive running was completed in order to prove the reliability of the new powerpack - particularly the gearbox and its integral steering units, which proved problematical from the outset. Indeed, the overall Mean Distance Between Failures for Challenger was just 109km, far short of the 350km of the General Staff Requirement. There were few problems with the gunnery and fire control systems, which were essentially identical to those of Chieftain. After further user trials and a four-day battlefield exercise on Salisbury Plain in October 1982, Challenger was accepted for service with the British Army (with certain provisos) on 14 December 1982.

(Above) The first production Challenger was delivered to the British Army on 16 March 1983. In June 1984 the MOD ordered an additional 64 tanks to equip a fifth armoured regiment in BAOR. Further orders followed in 1985 and 1986 to give a grand total of 420 Challenger MBTs, the last of which was delivered in late 1989.

There are three versions of Challenger (or, as it was later redesignated, Challenger 1): the Mark 1 (as illustrated), which was not fitted with TOGS (Thermal Observation & Gunnery System); the Mark 2, which is essentially the same as Mark 1 but with TOGS fitted; and the Mark 3, with a revised internal layout and many detail changes such as armoured charge bins.

(Above) The first Challenger regiment was The Royal Hussars, who received their first MBT on 12 April 1983 under conditions of strict secrecy; its every movement was under 24-hour armed guard. The regiment's A Sqn completed conversion by 23 September, and conducted the first troop trials between 10 October and 10 February 1984; these were codenamed Exercise Crimson Challenger - 'Crimson' after the colour of the regimental full dress trousers inherited from the 11th Hussars, the old 'Cherrypickers' of Light Brigade fame. Automotively the tank performed well; the Challengers covered 21,227km while consuming 181,000 litres of fuel, with each tank averaging 1,516km. Speeds of 70kph were achieved on roads, 50 kph over tracks and open fields, and 35kph across heavily broken ground, with the same speed in reverse. The higher speeds gave rise to noise and vibration problems, causing bolts and fittings to loosen as well as cracking of the idler wheels and sprocket rings. A casualty of the latter problem is shown here - a C Sqn Challenger on Exercise Lionheart 84.

(Left) The crew of a Challenger 1 Mk 2 of A Sqn, The Royal Dragoon Guards, replenish with HESH ammunition - High Explosive Squash Head - during gunnery training at Castlemartin; the projectile is painted blue to identify a SH/PRAC ('shush-P') practice round (see also page 14). The trooper in the background is passing a propellant bag charge to the loader inside the turret; the black plastic liner is discarded before stowage in the charge bins. (Simon Dunstan)

(Opposite top) With practice even the vast bulk of an MBT can be made to deceive the eye; here a Challenger 1 Mk 1 of C Sqn, The Royal Hussars, lies concealed in a 'hide' during Exercise Lionheart 84. The second unit to receive Challenger was 2nd Royal Tank Regiment, followed by 17th/21st Lancers and The Queen's Royal Irish Hussars.

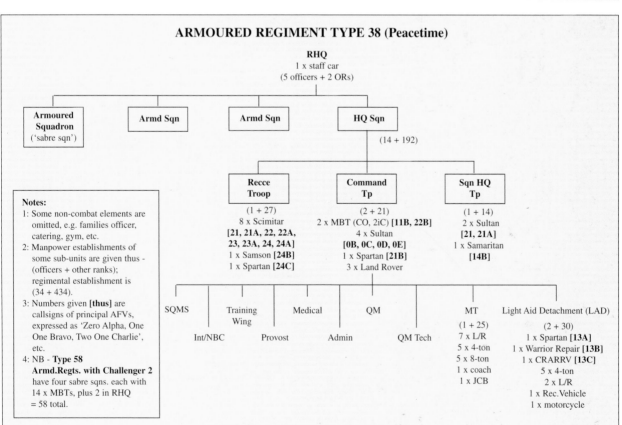

ARMOURED REGIMENT TYPE 38 (Peacetime)

RHQ
1 x staff car
(5 officers + 2 ORs)

Armoured Squadron ('sabre sqn')	**Armd Sqn**	**Armd Sqn**	**HQ Sqn**

HQ Sqn (14 + 192)

Recce Troop	**Command Tp**	**Sqn HQ Tp**
(1 + 27)	(2 + 21)	(1 + 14)
8 x Scimitar **[21, 21A, 22, 22A, 23, 23A, 24, 24A]**	2 x MBT (CO, 2iC) **[11B, 22B]**	2 x Sultan **[21, 21A]**
1 x Samson **[24B]**	4 x Sultan **[0B, 0C, 0D, 0E]**	1 x Samaritan **[14B]**
1 x Spartan **[24C]**	1 x Spartan **[21B]**	
	3 x Land Rover	

Notes:
1: Some non-combat elements are omitted, e.g. families officer, catering, gym, etc.
2: Manpower establishments of some sub-units are given thus - (officers + other ranks); regimental establishment is (34 + 434).
3: Numbers given **[thus]** are callsigns of principal AFVs, expressed as 'Zero Alpha, One One Bravo, Two One Charlie', etc.
4: NB - **Type 58 Armd.Regts. with Challenger 2** have four sabre sqns. each with 14 x MBTs, plus 2 in RHQ = 58 total.

SQMS	Training Wing	Medical	QM	MT	Light Aid Detachment (LAD)
				(1 + 25)	(2 + 30)
Int/NBC	Provost	Admin	QM Tech	7 x L/R	1 x Spartan **[13A]**
				5 x 4-ton	1 x Warrior Repair **[13B]**
				5 x 8-ton	1 x CRARRV **[13C]**
				1 x coach	5 x 4-ton
				1 x JCB	2 x L/R
					1 x Rec.Vehicle
					1 x motorcycle

(Above) The complexity and questionable ergonomics of the fire control system surrounding the gunner is shown to advantage in this view (looking forward and right from the loader's position, with the gun breech at bottom left). The gunner's principal Tank Laser Sight is at centre left, with the TOGS viewer to its right. Since the latter is offset at an angle, if the gunner observes through TOGS for any length of time during cross-country move- ment he soon acquires a considerable crick in the neck. Note the gunner's (grey, low centre) and commander's (white, upper right) hand controllers for gun transverse and elevation; these also incorporate the laser activation and Autolay button, together with the firing switch in the hand grip - a device which requires fine co-ordination, and presents difficulties for the left-handed. (Simon Dunstan)

(Opposite above) The commander sits on the right hand side of the turret with the gunner in front of and slightly below him. Here his seat is seen from the loader's position (looking backwards and left), with the TOGS Symbology Processing Unit (SPU, pronounced 'spew' - the main fire control computer) to the right of the seat as viewed here. The grey box above the SPU at top centre is the commander's Individual Display Unit or TOGS viewer, below which is the 'tunnel' where the commander stows his maps and personal belongings. The tray at the bottom of the photo is the normal position for the 'BV' or boiling vessel - that essential item in any British Army AFV. At top right is the ten-round ready rack for armour piercing projectiles, below which are the Clansman VRC 353 radios. (Simon Dunstan)

(Right) The view forward from below the breech of the 120mm main armament into the driver's compartment. In the centre is a stowage rack for High Explosive Squash Head rounds; all explosive rounds and propellant charges are stowed below the level of the turret ring. Above it is the driver's head rest for use when driving closed down. Each side of the driver's position is a liquid-lined ammunition propellant charge bin with clear plastic lids to show whether the bin holds a pair of half-charges for HESH rounds or a complete charge for armour piercing rounds. At bottom right of the photograph is the gunner's black firing pedal for the coaxial machine gun; at far left is the latter's flexible chute, known as the 'donkey dick', down which empty cases drop into a canvas bag. (Simon Dunstan)

(Opposite top) Fundamental to the design of the L11 120mm rifled tank gun is the use of three-piece ammunition: the projectile; a fully combustible propellant bag charge; and an igniter - a 'Tube Vent Electric'. Here, a loader of The Royal Dragoon Guards loads a bagged charge into the breech of the L11A7. It is not difficult to imagine the difficulty of this task when the tank is pitching erratically across country with the breech of the stabilized gun seemingly moving with a will of its own. At the same time the loader has to serve the coaxial machine gun; tune the radios; monitor the NBC system; view the battlefield through his rotating periscope; advise the commander of ammunition status and, last but not least, ensure that the BV is providing hot rations and constant cups of tea. (Simon Dunstan)

(Above) Despite the effectiveness of modern optical systems, few tank commanders will dispense with the most efficient sighting system of all - the Eyeball, Mark 1 - whether aided by binoculars or not. The commander of Challenger 1 has a Cupola AV No.32 which comprises a No.37 combined day/passive night sight (shown here with its protective cover open) and a ring of nine unity magnification vision blocks with their integral blade wipers (but no screen washers, which are often needed - note the mud spattered all over the turret roof). The cupola-mounted 7.62mm L37A2 machine gun is dismountable and has 300 rounds readily to hand in its fixed position which can be fired from under armour. From long experience of British tank designs, Challenger has a series of reversionary fire control devices whereby if one fails there are others to fall back on. The last resort is a simple No. 87 periscopic sight, visible here at bottom centre. (Simon Dunstan)

(Left) The loader of a Challenger 1 Mk 3 of The Queen's Royal Hussars demonstrates the loading procedure for the camera during gunnery training at the Glamoc ranges in Bosnia. (The tank is obviously not 'tactical' on this occasion - the trooper wears his beret rather than a helmet, and at top left HESH rounds can be seen temporarily stowed above the turret ring.) The yellow tip of the shells indicates high explosive; HESH ammunition is particular to the British Army, combining devastating effects against conventionally-armoured AFVs and a lethal high explosive charge against field fortifications, unarmoured vehicles and personnel in the open or in trenches. Note the blue DST practice rounds beyond the gun breech; and (far left) the tins of vent tube primers, which act as igniters for the combustible propellant charges.

The gunnery phase of Exercise Crimson Challenger, the initial troop trials, was conducted by The Royal Hussars between 14 and 22 November 1983 on Range 8B at Bergen Hohne. Challenger proved to be a more stable gun platform than Chieftain. The accuracy of APDS on commission firing was excellent, and the results of night firing using the commander's image intensifying sight were good, with 82 per cent of targets being hit. In general, the gun control equipment gave good service and the new Nd Yag tank laser sight was considered a great improvement over the earlier ruby type. A total of 1,747 120mm rounds was fired, including 140 APFSDS, 187 HESH, 20 Smoke, 608 DST and 732 SH/PRAC.

15

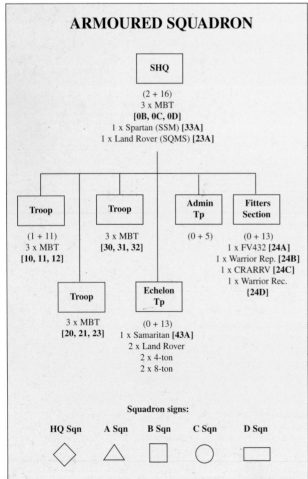

ARMOURED SQUADRON

SHQ

(2 + 16)
3 x MBT
[0B, 0C, 0D]
1 x Spartan (SSM) **[33A]**
1 x Land Rover (SQMS) **[23A]**

Troop

(1 + 11)
3 x MBT
[10, 11, 12]

Troop

3 x MBT
[30, 31, 32]

Admin Tp

(0 + 5)

Fitters Section

(0 + 13)
1 x FV432 **[24A]**
1 x Warrior Rep. **[24B]**
1 x CRARRV **[24C]**
1 x Warrior Rec.
{24D}

Troop

3 x MBT
[20, 21, 23]

Echelon Tp

(0 + 13)
1 x Samaritan **[43A]**
2 x Land Rover
2 x 4-ton
2 x 8-ton

Squadron signs:

HQ Sqn	A Sqn	B Sqn	C Sqn	D Sqn
◇	△	□	○	▭

(Above) Challengers of A Sqn, The Royal Dragoon Guards, are framed below the 120mm L11A7 gun of a companion tank as it approaches the firing line on the ranges at Castlemartin in South Wales. The gun barrel has a thermal sleeve to minimize distortion due to differential heating expansion characteristics during firing, which can cause loss of accuracy at long ranges. At the end of the barrel is the mirror housing of the Muzzle Reference System, which allows the gunner to check the exact alignment of his sights with the gun to maintain accuracy, particularly at long ranges. It is good practice to check the MRS after the firing of every few rounds - for the Lulworth range purist, probably after each round! (Simon Dunstan)

(Opposite top) 'Firing now!' - a Discarding Sabot Tracer (DST) practice round is discharged down range from a Challenger 1 Mk 2 of The Royal Dragoon Guards. The pole protruding above the turret is a telemetry device to assess hits and misses. A minimum of 44 projectiles can be carried in a Challenger 1, with a mixture of APFSDS (Armour Piercing Fin Stabilized Discarding Sabot), HESH (High Explosive Squash Head), and Smoke - a typical mix being 15 APFSDS, 25 HESH and 4 Smoke. There is a total of 42 bagged charge containers each holding one full AP charge or two HESH/Smoke half-charges. With their high velocity and flat trajectory, AP rounds are effective against armoured targets out to 3,000 metres; HESH rounds can be used against all types of targets out to 8,000 metres. (Simon Dunstan)

(Right) The tank second in line has just fired and its fume extractor - the cylindrical device midway down the barrel - is expelling the residual toxic propellant gases out of the muzzle rather than into the turret space when the breech is opened; in Second World War vintage tanks without this refinement turret crews often came near to asphyxia during prolonged firing. The red flag flying behind the commander's cupola denotes that the tank's weapons are loaded with live ammunition. The Challenger 1 has a coaxial 7.62mm L8A2 machine gun and a 7.62mm L37A2 machine gun at the commander's cupola for area defence. (Simon Dunstan)

(Left) 'One Zero', the troop leader's tank of 1 Troop, D Sqn, The King's Royal Hussars moves forward to begin a battle run on Range 9 at Bergen Hohne while Warrior AIFVs of 1st Bn, Coldstream Guards wait their turn in the background. Just visible on the side of the TOGS barbette is the black jerboa insignia of 4th Armoured Brigade; the inverted triangle squadron sign used by D Sqn, KRH is noteworthy - the standard geometric shape denoting D Sqn within a regiment is a horizontal rectangle. At the rear of the turret is the NBC environmental control system, which provides filtered air to each crewman when operating in contaminated conditions. (Simon Dunstan)

(Opposite bottom) As early as 1987 experiments were conducted by 17th/21st Lancers with Challengers fitted with additional fuel drums on the rear hull plate to increase the tank's range during long approach marches to the Inner German Border, more commonly known as the Iron Curtain. Although practicable they were deemed unsafe for use on public highways because of the fire risk in the event of collision; but the idea was resurrected during the Gulf War, and all the Challengers of 1st (UK) Armoured Division were so fitted. Many tanks retained these fittings on their return to Germany; and enterprising crews soon acquired fuel drums which were then modified to act as extra stowage containers for their

kit, as on this Challenger 1 Mk 3 of the squadron leader, D Sqn, The King's Royal Hussars on exercise in Germany. (Simon Dunstan)

(Below) Acting as enemy during Exercise First Crusade on Salisbury Plain, a Challenger 1 Mk 3 of D Sqn, The Queen's Royal Hussars uses dead ground to manoeuvre into a new fire position to engage the opposing AFVs of 1st (Mechanised) Brigade. Note the full-coloured regimental insignia on the TOGS barbette door; the dark patch cleaned of mud just below the registration plate 64KG97 is the black pig insignia of D Sqn, below which is the bridging classification of 70 tonnes in black

on a solid grey circle. A feature common to all British tanks since before the Second World War is a smoke grenade discharger cluster on each forward face of the turret, to produce an instant smokescreen behind which the tank can withdraw unobserved; Challenger has five-tube L8 clusters. The vehicle's headlights above each trackguard are masked by rubber rectangles cut from discarded mud flaps, to prevent tell-tale reflections. (Simon Dunstan)

(Opposite top) Emerging from a fold in the ground, a Challenger 1 Mk 2 of 1 Tp, D Sqn, The Royal Dragoon Guards engages the enemy during Exercise Phantom Bugle on Salisbury Plain, while a Warrior Artillery Observation Post directs air and artillery assets during the mock battle. Such a scenario is the essence of modern manoeuvre warfare, with combined arms groups acting in close concert to bring the maximum weight of firepower on to the enemy at the decisive moment. Following Gulf War experience, it is now common practice for Challenger crews to use TOGS during daylight hours and not just at night - hence the open TOGS barbette door. (Simon Dunstan)

(Opposite bottom) Engineer support is fundamental to the success of armoured warfare both in the offence and defence, so as to overcome obstacles when advancing and deny freedom of movement to the enemy when friendly forces are retiring. One of the simplest devices to maintain mobility, first used to support tanks at the battle of Cambrai in 1917, is the fascine. Originally constructed of brushwood bundles, fascines are now made up using PVC drainage pipes, which are both cheaper and lighter than natural materials. Mounted on the cradle of a Chieftain AVRE (Armoured Vehicle Royal Engineers), the fascine is dropped into anti-tank ditches or streams to allow the passage of other vehicles in the battlegroup - such as this Challenger 1 Mk 2 negotiating a wide gully during an exercise on Salisbury Plain.

(Above) A Challenger 1 Mk 2 of A Sqn, The King's Royal Hussars churns up the mud on the Bergen Hohne training area during Exercise Prairie Rat prior to deployment to BATUS in Canada. With its 1,200bhp V12 Perkins diesel engine, Challenger delivers approximately 800bhp at the sprockets - the remainder is consumed by the cooling group and electrical systems. For a tank with a combat weight of 62 tonnes this is quite adequate, and cross-country mobility is much enhanced by the Hydrogas suspension system. Comprising six units per side each providing 450mm of wheel movement, the system is highly efficient and, being independent, allows individual units to be replaced with relative ease following mine damage. (Simon Dunstan)

(Opposite) The Challenger Training Tank or CTT is the first purpose-designed driver training tank to see service with the British Army. Following a course of instruction on a simulator, the trainee driver progresses to the CTT for hands-on experience. As the turret systems account for almost two-thirds of the total cost of a modern Main Battle Tank, such vehicles have become commonplace in all Western armies. Designed by Vickers Defence Systems in a fixed-price contract of £18m, the first CTT was delivered to the British Army in 1990, and 17 are currently in service at the Royal Armoured Corps Centre at Bovington, Dorset and at the School of Electrical & Mechanical Engineers (SEME) at Bordon, Hampshire.

The hull of the CTT is identical to that of the MBT, but with a non-rotating observation and control cabin for the driving instructor and up to four other students. The cabin is fabricated of welded steel plate and has toughened glass windows all round, an entry/exit door on each side and two emergency escape hatches in the roof. The instructor is provided with an instrument panel featuring LED indicator lamps which duplicate the warning lights displayed to the driver, together with an indicator of the gear range selected. This allows him not only to monitor the performance of the student, but also to create warnings of automotive faults such as low oil pressure or a blocked air filter on the driver's instrument panel, to see how he reacts to different situations. The driver, for his part, is provided with a simulated gun position indicator, the direction of which is also controlled by the instructor, so that an unwary student may find himself notionally knocking down trees or street lights. In case of necessity the instructor is also provided with an emergency brake lever and the facility to exercise an emergency stop by means of a cut-out switch. (Simon Dunstan)

(Above) Mines remain a potent threat to AFVs, and countermeasures are vital to maintain the mobility of the battlegroup. Although used by Soviet forces for many years, mine ploughs have only recently been adopted by Western armies in significant numbers. This Challenger is fitted with a Pearson Engineering Full-Width Mine Plough (FWMP) which, as its name implies, clears mines across the full width of the vehicle. This device is more normally employed by armoured engineer vehicles than gun tanks. On the rear quarter of this Challenger is a Pathfinder marking system, which is operated from under armour; it places marker poles at predetermined intervals to one or either side of the vehicle, delineating a mine-clear path for following vehicles.

(**Above & opposite top**) A neatly-stowed Challenger Armoured Repair & Recovery Vehicle (CRARRV) at the School of Electrical & Mechanical Engineers awaits its quota of REME students prior to recovery exercises on Bordon Heath in Hampshire.

From the outset the existing Chieftain ARRV had considerable difficulties in supporting the Challenger MBT in the field, and in 1984 tenders were sought from industry for a recovery vehicle based on Challenger. The design by Vickers Defence Systems was chosen for development in a fixed-price contract for 30 vehicles, and the first six prototypes were completed in 1987. After exhaustive trials, including a programme of some 1,300 maximum load, full-line main winch pulls - the equivalent of 65 years' worth of peacetime usage for one vehicle - the production run of 26 CRARRVs began in 1989. It was accepted for service with the British Army in June 1990, with four of the prototypes being modified to production standards to fulfil the initial contract for 30 vehicles; a further 50 have subsequently been purchased. (Simon Dunstan)

(**Right**) The CRARRV was soon nicknamed 'Rhino' by its REME crews, and this subsequently became its official name. The Rhino has a basic crew of three comprising commander, driver and radio operator, all of whom are REME tradesmen, with seats for up to two more tradesmen. British Army doctrine demands that many repair tasks for MBTs must be undertaken in the field. Accordingly Rhino is provided with a comprehensive range of equipment including welding and cutting bottles and compressed air tools, as well as an Atlas AK6000 M8 hydraulic crane capable of lifting a complete Challenger power-pack at a weight of 5,488kg. The multi-purpose front-mounted blade can act as an earth anchor, 'dozer blade or crane stabiliser. The CRARRV can tow vehicles weighing up to 70 tonnes at speeds of up to 35kph. Here, a Rhino of OPFOR (Opposing Forces) recovers a broken-down Chieftain of 1RTR during an exercise on Salisbury Plain. (Tim Neate)

(Above) The power train of Challenger 1 is an integrated powerpack comprising engine, cooling system with fans at the rear, and transmission. The engine is a Condor CV12 TCA 12-cylinder 60v direct injection four stroke diesel compression ignition of 26.1 litres rated at 1,200bhp (895kw), built by Perkins Engines of Shrewsbury. The transmission comprises a TN37 epicyclic gearbox with four forward gears and three reverse, incorporating an integral STN37 hydrostatic steering system as well as the oil-immersed multiplate main brakes. The photograph shows the complete powerpack, with a REME fitter providing scale. The main engine takes up less than half the total volume of the powerpack, the radiators and oil coolers lying flat above the transmission. Typical of British tanks, there is an auxiliary Generator Unit Engine to charge the batteries and allow quieter and more economical radio watch. With the help of quick-release connectors the powerpack can be replaced in approximately one hour. Each powerpack costs about £150,000. (Simon Dunstan)

(Left) A Challenger 1 Mk 3 of The King's Royal Hussars, with turret traversed to the rear, waits its turn for refuelling on the Bergen Hohne training area (note the insignia of the former 20th Hussars on the smoke grenade stowage box). With a fuel capacity of 1,797 litres, Challenger 1 has a range of approximately 450km at a top speed of almost 65kph (40kph across country) thanks to the highly efficient Hydrogas suspension system. The rear hull plate has attachment points for supplementary fuel drums, raised above the level of the engine decks to allow gravity feeding of diesel into the main fuel tanks; these give an extra 100 kilometres of range. (Simon Dunstan)

(Left) The complexity of modern MBTs demands regular maintenance procedures; here, hidden from aerial view, Challenger crews of The King's Royal Hussars carry out routine maintenance prior to an exercise, from lubrication of the suspension units to cleaning the 120mm main armament. (Simon Dunstan)

(Right) Characteristically the turrets are at 90 degrees to the hulls, to allow access to the engine compartment; note 4th Armd.Bde. sign on TOGS barbette. One criticism of Challenger has been that it is extremely difficult to perform any real maintenance to the powerpack without removing the complete engine decks, a task which requires a crane. Accordingly, it is inevitable that some crews carry out only perfunctory checks of oil and coolant levels, which has resulted in reduced reliability. (Simon Dunstan)

Back in the 1980s a chronic shortage of spare parts and an ever-decreasing allocation of track mileage so reduced the availability for action of the Challenger fleet in BAOR that it sometimes fell to below 20 per cent - hardly a serious deterrent to the Warsaw Pact. Happily, the figures achieved with the wartime levels of support enjoyed by 1st (UK) Armd.Div. in the Gulf War demonstrated Challenger's basic reliability. (Simon Dunstan)

(Opposite top) After the loss of the vast desert training grounds in Libya in 1969, the British Army required somewhere of similar scale, and decided upon the wide open rolling prairies of the province of Alberta, Canada. Covering an area of almost 2,500 square kilometres, the British Army Training Unit Suffield (BATUS) allows battlegroup training using all types of live ammunition in highly realistic field training exercises known collectively as 'Medicine Man'. There are six 'Med Man' exercises each year, held between the spring and autumn as the bitter cold precludes effective training during the winter. Each 'Med Man' costs approximately £16 million. These Challengers are manned by The Queen's Royal Lancers during a 'Med Man' deployment in 1994. The red metal plates above the tanks' cupolas indicate that their weapons are loaded with live ammunition.

(Left) At BATUS a battlegroup comprises two Challenger squadrons each of 12 tanks (designated 1st and 2nd Armoured Squadrons); and two Warrior companies each with 14 armoured infantry fighting vehicles, as well as a reconnaissance platoon of eight Scimitar CVR(T) and a battery of six AS90s. The battlegroup can be configured as either tank- or infantry-heavy, with the respective arm being in command, while additional support is provided by Royal Engineers, Royal Electrical & Mechanical Engineers and Army Air Corps assets.

Here a Challenger 1 Mk 2 of 1st Armd.Sqn. (identifiable by the white-painted fume extractor) thunders across the prairie. The AFVs at BATUS are painted in the characteristic camouflage scheme of green over sand yellow which is also applied to OPFOR AFVs in the United Kingdom, with simple white-painted tactical callsigns. The white circular device above the cupola indicates that no weapons are loaded and the laser rangefinder is switched off to conform with the strict safety measures enforced at BATUS. Note the rubber bung in the muzzle of the 120mm gun to stop dust and foreign matter fouling the rifling of the barrel. On operations such an item is disposable and is blown away when the gun is fired.

(Above) Because of the intensive nature of 'Med Man' exercises the tanks at BATUS undertake some of the highest track mileages of the Challenger fleet. Accordingly they require regular maintenance both by the crews and REME personnel. The long-standing problem of the crew's difficulty in lifting the heavy armoured engine decking to carry out first-line maintenance has been overcome by the addition of a counter-sprung torsion bar. This allows the engine decking to be raised exposing the oil filters, auxiliary engine, and fuel injection pump, as well as facilitating oil and coolant level checks. Here, 'Two Two Bravo' of the 2nd Armd. Sqn. of the resident BATUS armoured inventory undergoes maintenance in the workshops at Camp Crowfoot, with an AS90 155mm self-propelled howitzer in the background.

(**Right**) This photograph of a Challenger 1 Mk 2 of the BATUS 1st Armd.Sqn. shows to advantage the TOGS, and the white painted V on the turret roof, which is known as the 'forty-fives'. Visible through both the commander's and gunner's sights, the 'forty-fives' are aligned with either the right or left front trackguard, as ordained by range controllers to determine safe arcs of fire when using live ammunition. Note the Thermal Imager Sensor Head (TISH) inside the open door of the TOGS barbette.

(**Above**) The ability to manoeuvre rapidly to a new fire position while presenting the heaviest - frontal - armour to the enemy increases the chances of survival significantly. Challenger's high speed reverse gear ratio allows it to retire backwards at 65kph, which can on occasion prove alarming to other exercise participants nearby. Here, festooned with helmets and stowage, a Challenger 1 reverses out of a concealing dust cloud. Note the horizontal pole attached to the back of the turret behind the water jerrycans. This has a rear-facing blue light cluster at each end to aid night formation-keeping. It also shows range safety staff which way the turret is pointing, and thus that it is within set parameters when firing live ammunition - a night shoot is the most difficult part of an exercise to control safely. Note also the empty OMD 80 engine oil container beside the registration plate. With the top and bottom cut out, such tins are used as portable lavatories to be placed over a prepared hole in the ground; this is preferable to sim-

ply squatting in an undignified Gallic manner in the middle of the endless prairie.

Each 'Med Man' lasts for 23 days, involving both live firing and various Tactical Engagement Simulation Exercises. During a TESEX sensors are attached to both men and vehicles which are activated by special laser adaptions to opposition weapons. Any recorded hits oblige infantrymen to lie down and remove their helmets to feign death or injury, while vehicles are rendered immobile or 'destroyed' depending on the severity of the 'hit'.

At BATUS the OPFOR comprises vehicles of the CVR(T) range configured to simulate the characteristics of Russian AFVs; thus a Scorpion becomes a Salamander or T-80, and a Spartan is a Sturgeon or BMP-2. Being fast and compact, like most Russian designs, the OPFOR vehicles are difficult to engage and, as OPFOR troops are resident at BATUS and highly familiar with the terrain, they can prove deadly foes in these very realistic engagements.

Although the FV4030 series was originally developed for Iran, the tank was not - contrary to statements elsewhere - specially configured for desert conditions. Indeed, the cooling group of the Condor powerpack absorbs a considerable proportion of total energy, and in high summer temperatures at BATUS this can reduce the real output at the sprocket to levels on a par with Chieftain. Gulf War experience has led to the fitting of an improved air filter which gives better acceleration and a higher top speed. Even so, the fine prairie dust (see opposite, top) reduces the lifespan of filters far below the manufacturer's projection.

(**Right**) During the late 1980s the rising Green movement in West Germany demanded greater ecological protection, placing serious constraints on the level and realism of BAOR battle-group exercises. Ironically, with the collapse of the Warsaw Pact former communist regimes were quick to realise the monetary value of their own training grounds. Since 1996 the British Army has used the Drawsko-Pomorskie Training Area (DPTA) in Poland for combined arms tactical combat manoeuvre training. Exercise Uhlan Eagle 96, conducted between 30 August and 18 September by elements of 7th Armd.Bde., involved the Warriors of 1st Bn, Royal Highland Fusiliers, and the full complement of 38 Challengers of 2RTR; the latter are shown here lined up at the outset - note the natural foliage camouflage, no longer allowed in Germany.

(Above) Troops of 1RHF dismount from their Warrior supported by a Challenger 1 Mk 2 of 2RTR. Uhlan Eagle 96 involved more than 3,500 personnel with 490 AFVs and almost 750 support vehicles, which were deployed to Poland in a combination of some 18 trains for the AFVs and 30 road convoys.

(Opposite top) A sight to cause apprehension to every experienced soldier - young officers arguing over a map ... here, a group of them from 2RTR and 40th Regt Royal Artillery prior to Uhlan Eagle 96, in front of the Challengers of the Command Troop of RHQ and an RA Warrior OPV (Observation Post Vehicle) of 40 RA. The two Challengers are named after the greatest battle honours of the RTR: the CO's tank is CAMBRAI and his second-in-command has ARRAS. The other tanks in 2RTR are named after those of the original companies of the Tank Corps during the Great War. The present 2RTR - formed from the amalgamation of 2 and 3RTR - comprises B, C,

E and F Sqns (F being Headquarters); these letters correspond to those of the original companies, and apart from the Command Troop their tank names begin with the appropriate letter.

(Right) A Challenger 1 Mk 2 of 2RTR carefully negotiates a triple-span, triple-tier Bailey bridge (the first to be constructed by the Royal Engineers for many years) across the Drawa River, which in places is over 100 metres wide.

With the closure of the Soltau training area, where generations of BAOR soldiers had endured the dusty heat of summer, the mud and freezing rain of autumn, and the truly Siberian cold of winter, the remaining manoeuvre areas in Germany have become uncomfortably crowded and predictable. The purpose of exercises in DPTA is to practice high intensity combined arms operations at brigade and battlegroup level in typical North-West European terrain. Although no live ammuni-

tion is now used on DPTA, it has in fact been used for military training since 1943, first by the Wehrmacht and post-war by the Warsaw Pact as a live firing range; numerous tank hulks litter the heath, and some of the erstwhile pop-up targets look suspiciously like Challengers.

Unlike BATUS, DPTA has numerous natural obstacles and watercourses which require extensive engineer support to negotiate, while the REME are kept busy recovering tanks bogged in marshy ground. Although the terrain is somewhat restrictive to the Challengers, Warrior has once more displayed its excellent mobility; the infantry have to dismount repeatedly to clear the numerous obstacles which, although tiring, makes for first class training. (It is hard to find a silver lining in the all-pervasive clouds of mosquitoes, however.) The dense woods and the extremely dark nights make navigation a real challenge, with the constant danger of driving into old tank scrapes and ditches.

DPTA is over 400sq/km in

area, and virtually unpopulated except for range staff and a few forestry workers - although any section attack may come across a determined Polish mushroom-picker, often with his parked 'Polski Fiat', in places that an AFV crew would think twice about negotiating. Equally determined was the local madame, who imported reinforcements in the oldest profession from Warsaw and Gdansk in the expectation that British officers and senior NCOs would avail themselves of her services (as had all previous users of the training area). She was dumbfounded to learn that they remained in the field with their troops throughout the exercise, and became so incensed at the lack of trade that she demanded an interview with the brigadier commanding.

Active Service:
The Gulf 1990-91

The Iraqi invasion of Kuwait on 2 August 1990 prompted a concerted United Nations response against the regime of Saddam Hussein, creating a coalition of disparate nations to counter such blatant aggression. Among the first countries to provide forces was Britain, which despatched to Saudi Arabia the 7th Armoured Brigade Group comprising two armoured regiments, each with 58 Challengers, and an armoured infantry battalion equipped with Warrior - 1st Bn, The Staffordshire Regiment.

(Opposite top) Here a Challenger 1 Mk 3 in its new desert livery disembarks from a Landing Ship Logistic at Al Jubayl; the cross of St Andrew on the TOGS barbette indicates that it belongs to The Royal Scots Dragoon Guards. (SCOTS DG)

(Left) Flying the flag of Ulster, Challengers of The Queen's Royal Irish Hussars soon after landing in Saudi Arabia, where the temperature hovered around the 100˚F mark. The tanks were soon moved to Shed 4 where they underwent a programme of 'Quayside Modifications'. Most of these were designed to enhance performance in desert conditions, such as improved air filters, maintenance-free batteries, and a cooling fan for the gun control equipment; essential modifications were also made to the auxiliary engine. One squadron of Challengers was modified every 24 hours by 7th Armoured Workshop REME, supported by technical personnel from manufacturers such as Vickers, Barr & Stroud, Marconi and Perkins. (QRIH)

(Above) A Challenger 1 Mk 3 of B Sqn, The Royal Scots Dragoon Guards is refuelled from a Bedford UBRE during an early regimental exercise. On 24 October 1990 the first tanks were deployed to the desert in the area of Al Fadili, to begin training at troop and then at squadron level until regimental and finally brigade-size exercises were undertaken. The 7th Armoured Brigade Group was declared operational on 16 November and came under the command of 1st (US) Marine Division as its heavy armour element.

Like their predecessors of the Second World War 'Desert Rats', the tank crews soon realized the difficulty of navigating in such featureless terrain; but whereas their forebears had to rely on a sun compass, which could only be used effectively at a distance from the magnetic influence of the vehicle, modern technology provided the answer with the issue of GPS (Global Positioning System) equipment. This device, be it Magellan or Trimble, gives an exact grid reference, which allows an armoured formation to manoeuvre freely and precisely so as to attack the enemy in force from the least expected quarter. (SCOTS DG)

(Opposite top) The British contingent was increased to divisional strength with the arrival of 4th Armoured Brigade and other supporting elements over the Christmas 1990 period. Further modifications were made to Challenger, with the addition of Chobham armour panels along its sides, and an array of ERA (Explosive Reactive Armour) blocks over the glacis plate and lower hull front. The latter are shown here being fitted to a Challenger 1 Mk 3 of 14th/20th King's Hussars during an NBC alert, making an onerous task even more difficult in the desert sun. The frontal aspect was further protected by a supplementary armour plate around the driver's position.

The additional armour rendered Challenger virtually immune to all Iraqi infantry anti-tank weapons over the front and sides. The only Challenger to be made immobile by gunfire during 'The Hundred Hours War' was a tank of the 14th/20th which was hit in one of the rear-mounted final drive housings by a 30mm round mistakenly fired by a following Warrior. The tank was rapidly repaired, and continued in service to the end of hostilities.

(Left) Among other modifications fitted to Challenger was a smoke-generating device, similar to that used by Soviet tanks for many years, which creates a smokescreen by injecting diesel fuel into the exhaust outlets. The dense cloud of smoke was intended to mask the movement of friendly forces from Iraqi observation but, because of the thermal imaging sights of the TOGS system, Challenger crews could still detect and engage targets through it. Modified from the fuel pump of a Bedford 4-ton truck, the device was somewhat makeshift and caused the stowed gear on the outside of the tank to be tainted with diesel fuel - and on occasion, to catch fire. Accordingly it was usually fitted to the tank of the 'junior callsign' within the unit. Due to the nature of the fighting, it was not used during the ground offensive. (QRIH)

(Above) The supplementary Chobham armour side panels and the ERA blocks of the nose armour are shown to advantage on these Challengers of 3 Tp, A Sqn, 14th/20th King's Hussars (note the three rings of 3 Troop on the fume extractor, and the name AARDVARK just visible on 'Three One') during final training before the land offensive. The configuration of the ERA blocks on the lower glacis and toe plate forms a pointed shape for optimum ballistic protection and to minimise bellying in soft sand. The heaviest Chobham armour panels provide further protection to those areas where the ammunition propellant charges are stored. On the Mark 3 model of Challenger 1 these are contained in armoured charge bins. For this reason only the Mark 3 model was deployed on Operation Granby because of its greater survivability. This feature, together with the supplementary armour, made Challenger 1 the most heavily protected contemporary MBT extant.

A graphic example of the benefits of total air superiority, as elements of 4th Armd.Bde. are aligned for a commemorative aerial photograph shortly before the land offensive. Such a deployment is anathema in a war zone under normal circumstances.

During Operation Granby, 4th Armd.Bde. comprised the 58 Challengers of 14th/20th King's Hussars and the 108 Warriors of 1st Bn, The Royal Scots and 3rd Bn, The Royal Regiment of Fusiliers. Following the tank - heavy 7th Armd.Bde. through the

breech created in the Iraqi front lines by the US 1st Infantry Division (Mechanised) - 'The Big Red One' - the infantry - heavy 4th Armd. Bde. followed the southern axis of the advance of 1st (UK) Armd.Div.; in a series of intense night battles

they eliminated a succession of Iraqi formations in prepared positions, which were codenamed after metals, e.g. Bronze, Brass, Steel and Tungsten.

(Above) For much of 'The Hundred Hours War' the weather was foul, and visibility was measured in metres through a combination of lashing rain, sand storms and, as the armoured formations charged into Kuwait, the dense black smoke of hundreds of burning oil wells. However, the Challengers of 1st (UK) Armd.Div. used their superior thermal imaging sights to full advantage. Although their performance was slightly degraded by the appalling weather, these enabled the battlegroups to overwhelm the Iraqi positions at night or in conditions of limited visibility before the enemy could react. Within short order the Iraqis proved incapable of maintaining a coherent defence, and on contact they usually decided that surrender was the most sensible course of action. More often than not they had been deserted by their officers and left with inadequate supplies of food and water. At the forefront of the attack by 7th Armd.Bde. for much of the offensive were the Challengers - like 'Four Zero' pictured here - of D Sqn, The Queen's Royal Irish Hussars, who in the best traditions of the cavalry were to cut the Basra Road minutes before the cease-fire was declared at 0800 hours on 28 February 1991.

(Opposite top) The Challenger Armoured Repair & Recovery Vehicle - CRARRV - was scheduled to enter service with the British Army in April 1991, but on account of the Gulf War the first four production vehicles were rushed to Saudi Arabia on 24 September 1990 to support 7th Armoured Brigade Group. A further eight were deployed subsequently, and ten were divided between 4th and 7th Armd.Bdes. with the other two being held in War Maintenance Reserve.

Although not attached to any particular armoured regiment, this CRARRV sports a cross of St Andrew sticker (just left of the winching block) which suggests that it has supported The Royal Scots Dragoon Guards. SCOTS DG had the misfortune to have four tanks mired in the *sabkah* on one occasion; this is an area of soft sand with the consistency of wet cement, under a hard crust which is unable to bear the weight of a tank. Early recovery attempts by a Chieftain ARRV and an American M88A1 proved futile, but the CRARRV extracted all four in short order in its first ever operational recovery task.

(Right) CRARRV number 70KG71, named MOYRA, of the Forward Repair Group of 4th Armd.Bde. (note the black jerboa insignia well forward on the hull side) gives assistance to 14th/20th King's Hussars shortly after the end of the Gulf War. The telescopic-boom Atlas crane has a lifting capacity of 6.5 tonnes, which is used primarily for exchanging powerpacks - a task which takes approximately 60 minutes. The CRARRV is fitted with the more efficient David Brown TN54 automatic gearbox (as is Challenger 2), which allows improved low speed manoeuvrability over the previous TN37. During 'The Hundred Hours War' the CRARRVs provided comprehensive support to the armoured formations, and were instrumental in maintaining an availability rate for the Challenger MBTs of over 90 per cent during the land campaign. (David Rowlands)

Active Service: Bosnia since 1996

In 1991-92 the former Republic of Yugoslavia disintegrated; in the aftermath of the collapse of Communism the long-suppressed mutual hostilities between its different communities flared into a chaotic series of civil wars. These were pursued with such savagery that early in 1992 the appalled international community felt obliged to insert into Bosnia, then the arena for the worst atrocities, a United Nations Protection Force (UNPROFOR). A major British contingent demonstrated courage and professionalism over the next three years; but UNPROFOR was handicapped by a confused chain of command and a very restricted mandate from the UNO. It quickly became clear that there were no 'good guys and bad guys' in this medieval scenario; all the factions cynically committed cruelties and treacheries, quickly learning how to exploit the limitations of UNPROFOR's rules of engagement.

Temporarily exhausted, the various Serbian, Croatian and Bosnian factions reluctantly agreed to a US-sponsored ceasefire under the Dayton peace accords in December 1995. Simultaneously the UN Security Council handed over responsibility for policing this ceasefire to a new NATO-led Implementation Force (IFOR) with a much more robustly defined mission. Over the past three years a rotating force of Challenger tanks have provided one of the major deterrent elements of the British contingent. At the time of writing the focus of tension in former Yugoslavia has moved to the Serbian province of Kosovo; the outcome of NATO air operations is uncertain, and an open-ended deployment of British troops to this tortured corner of Europe seems all too likely.

(**Below**) Operation Resolute: on 10 January 1996, A & B Sqns of The Queen's Royal Hussars moved from the Croatian port of Split to Kupres in Bosnia. In a 24-hour round trip the Scammell Commanders of 3rd Tank Transporter Sqn, Royal Logistic Corps, carried the 28 MBTs and three CRARRVs over the Dynaric Mountains during a fortunate break in the bleak winter weather. During its tour 3rd Sqn RLC moved 28,000 tonnes of AFVs and motored one million kilometres. Passing through burning Bosnian villages, the convoys were quick to witness the barbarity of civil war - an impression reinforced by the welcome extended by some locals, who would shoot contaminated hypodermic needles through air-rifles at passing IFOR troops.

(**Right**) The Challenger 1 Mk 3 of 1st Troop leader (Lt Greenwood) of B Sqn, QRH, was the first tank to be unloaded at Kupres, at which desolate spot they were fuelled and bombed-up with ammunition pre-positioned in ISO containers. Initially their main role was to act as a blunt demonstration of IFOR's will and capability to implement the Dayton accords. If any of the factions were to be foolish enough to attack IFOR openly the tanks could be quickly fitted with the same up-armouring package as applied during the Gulf War; enough kits for all the IFOR Challengers are stored in theatre.

(**Below right**) Each squadron had an attached troop drawn from D Sqn, QRH, whose 'black pig' is painted below the nose registration of DESPERATE, the Mk 3 of Lt Sutherland during the first patrol outside Mrkonjic Grad on 13 January. Other markings include the regimental insignia on the TOGS barbette door; and on its side the white fern of New Zealand, marking the comradeship between the NZ Division and the old 3rd Hussars following El Alamein in 1942.

As if the Army did not already produce enough of them, Bosnia has given birth to a whole new 'alphabet soup' of acronyms. The first task of IFOR troops was to create Zones of Separation (ZOS) between the Former Warring Factions (FWF). Accordingly the two QRH squadrons were widely dispersed: A Sqn was based in an abandoned bus depot near Bosanski Petrovac; and B Sqn moved to Mrkonjic Grad, where 2nd and 3rd Tps worked with 1st Bn, The Royal Regiment of Fusiliers (1RRF) in their Saxon APCs, while 1st and 4th Tps were attached to the Warrior battalion at Sanski Most - 2nd Bn, The Light Infantry (2LI).

(Above) 180 tonnes of Challengers make a formidable roadblock at the 'White Fang' checkpoint on Route Phoenix between Sanski Most and Prijedor. Here 'Zero Bravo', the Challenger 1 Mk 3 of the squadron leader of B Sqn (but commanded on 17 January by Sgt Balmforth), is carefully

driven past the Portakabin used for meetings organized by IFOR between local factions for low-level negotiations and the exchange of prisoners, hostages or corpses. It remains standard practice to use TOGS even during daylight; note the TISH behind the open TOGS door. Beside the Union Flag flying from the radio antenna is the White Rose pennant of Yorkshire, which indicates the provenance of Sgt Balmforth. Orange tape lines the route to remind traffic to keep to the road because of the danger of mines.

(Opposite top) With their auxiliary generators running, tanks of 1st Tp, B Sqn, QRH stand ready at the inhospitable checkpoint known as 'Cold Hussar', situated on the second highest mountain in Bosnia near the village of Mliniste on the southern edge of an area known as 'The Anvil' in NW Bosnia. Hemmed in by steep slopes and dense pine forest, 'Cold Hussar' was an important IEBL (Inter-Entity Boundary Line) between the Serbs and the

Croatian-Muslim Federation. A troop was stationed there at all times to guard against the illegal passage of troops, hostages and arms. Being at least one hour away from Squadron HQ in good weather, and up to six during heavy snow, 'Cold Hussar' proved a surprisingly popular posting. Troops were left to use their own initiative to contain the more outrageous behaviour of the locals, such as kidnapping passing civilians of another ethnic group and attempting to exchange them for their own prisoners of war.

(Right) The Challengers of QRH extended their patrols until they had managed to negotiate some 80 per cent of the roads and tracks within their Area of Operational Responsibility (AOR) - this despite the initial assessment of many staff officers and infantrymen that 'the tanks wouldn't be able to go anywhere' and would be 'reduced to roadblocks'. All IFOR tanks and military vehicles are confined to roads and specific tracks because

of the ever-present mine threat - indeed, no routes are tried until they have been checked by engineers and cleared if necessary. Here, Cpl Fright keeps a lookout at the loader's hatch of his Challenger 1 Mk 3 of 2 Tp, B Sqn during a patrol in February 1996. The only modification to Challenger in such weather was the removal of four track pads in every 14 to increase grip on the icy roads; however, a compromise has to be made between adhesion and damage to the road surface. Several Challengers have performed alarming 180 and 360 degree pirouettes, but fortunately only a few have actually slid off the road, presenting interesting recovery tasks for the CRARRVs of the Light Aid Detachment.

(Opposite top) 'One One Bravo', the tank of the CO, Lt Col Nigel Beer, pauses during a patrol on the road to Klujc; note the auxiliary fuel drums with their ends removed to make extra stowage containers for the crew's kit. Since authority passed from the UN to IFOR on 21 December 1995 national flags have once more been prominently displayed, both out of pride and for quick identification between IFOR contingents. Note the ruined house in the left background - it is possible to motor for scores of kilometres in Bosnia without seeing a single building with its roof intact. In Serbo-Croat the contemporary euphemism for looting translates as 'shopping'.

There have been several occasions when Challengers employed on Operation Resolute/Lodestar have deployed in force to counter provocation by various factions. One such was the advance of an armoured brigade of the Muslim V Corps against the Bosnian Croats in the disputed town of Kulen Vakuf. Within an hour of receiving movement orders blocking posi-

tions had been established by A Sqn, QRH, supported by AS90 self-propelled howitzers, attack helicopters, the Milan ATGWs and mortars of the infantry as well as the QRH Recce Troop. The Muslim armour came to within 6km before being detected by a Scimitar of Recce Troop, which caused the column to halt. The corps commander, Gen Dudakovic, went further forward in his Mercedes staff car; but on seeing the Challengers he withdrew his forces forthwith.

(Left) The success of IFOR in persuading the FWF to respect the Dayton accords allowed the emphasis of operations to be shifted to supporting the civil population in rebuilding the devastated infrastructure of Bosnia/Herzegovina (designated G-5 or 'hearts and minds' operations). One of the most powerful tools in the battlegroup's inventory was the CRARRV, which can be employed for a multitude of tasks - here the HQ Squadron CRARRV is clearing debris at Klujc, site of the Battlegroup HQ. The QRH deployed with three CRARRVs - one with each

sabre squadron and the other with HQ Sqn and the main LAD; one or two more drawn from theatre assets were often attached to the widely dispersed units, these originally being provided by 3rd Bn REME and subsequently by 6th Battalion. These units also had to support the AS90s of the Royal Artillery, and the Chieftain AVREs and bridgelayers of the Royal Engineers. Any breakdown of a heavy AFV on the narrow roads of Bosnia could cause utter chaos, and it was essential to have recovery support always close at hand.

(Above) The QRH deployed to Bosnia with 28 Challenger 1 Mk 3s: A & B Sqns. with 12 each, two in Battlegroup HQ and two in reserve. C Sqn replaced A Sqn in March 1996, typically inheriting an AOR of about 1,200sq/km; extensive patrolling gave each Challenger an average monthly road running in excess of 400km. By the end of the tour each MBT had motored an average of 2,400km, as against 8,000km for CVR(T) - the equivalent of a year's track mileage in

Germany; while the battlegroup consumed 760,855 litres of diesel fuel and 145,276 of petrol.

With the coming of spring it was possible to build more comfortable quarters; initially many Hussars had to sleep under canvas in temperatures as low as -28°C, sharing their bivvies with rats of such determination that the pouches of the 95 Pattern Combat webbing proved unequal to their appetite for 'battle bennies' or any scrap of food. Here a D Sqn Challenger on attachment to B Sqn stands outside the living accommodation at 'Cold Hussar', in company with a pair of CVR(T) Sabres of The Light Dragoons, during May 1996.

47

(Opposite top) At the outset of a patrol, callsign 'Three Zero' leaves the tank park near Mrkonjic Grad with Lt Sutherland and Cpl Garner in the turret. B Squadron's base here was named Balaklava Camp; that of A Sqn (and latterly C) at Bosanski Petrovac was Alamein Camp - today's much-amalgamated British Army regiments have no shortage of battle honours to select for such purposes. Before the war Mrkonjic Grad was a thriving town with a population of 27,000; when the QRH arrived in January 1996 only six people were living among the devastation. However, by the end of the tour it was again bustling as people returned to their homes; such is the return on the expenditure of blood and treasure in support of UN peace-keeping operations.

These crewmen are wearing the Combat Soldier 95 (CS95) ensemble uniform, designed on the layering principle whereby single components make a suitable lightweight uniform for the tropics, and build up to the maximum of eight layers for Arctic conditions. While the latter is thermally efficient it can be too bulky inside an AFV; so a new all-black padded tanksuit has been issued for use in Bosnia.

(Left) The two dates that were fundamental to the implementation of the Dayton accord were D+90, when Zones of Separation were created between the warring factions; and D+120, when their troops were obliged to return to barracks. In the B Sqn area of operations D+120 was uneventful; but C Sqn were faced by a serious situation at the Muslim town of Kulen Vakuf, from which Bosnian Croat forces refused to withdraw. Accordingly, C Sqn took up blocking positions to prevent reinforcement by any party, while B Sqn was called upon to assist. Here, the B Sqn CRARRV and the LAD deploy for the move to Alamein Camp on D+120. Fortunately the Bosnian Croats backed down and confrontation was averted.

Note that the crew of this Rhino are wearing the new black 'Dew' tanksuits with fur fabric collars; what The Royal Tank Regiment thinks of cavalrymen sporting such an outfit remains unknown ...

(Above) With the QRH cap badge prominently on display, L/Cpl Nick Flack checks the boresight of the L11A7 120mm main armament of his Challenger 1 Mk 3 of 3 Tp, C Sqn at the Glamoc gunnery ranges during May 1996. Boresighting is the means whereby the gunner's sight is aligned to the axis of the gun barrel to ensure accuracy. The gunner lays onto an aiming mark at a range of 1,000m and makes corrections as determined by the man viewing through the boresight onto the chosen target before adjusting his sight graticule. The commander's sight, auxiliary sight, and the thermal sensor of TOGS can be adjusted accordingly. Challenger 79KF56 lacks a front wing, mudguard and towing hook - the result of a steering failure on a narrow mountain road which caused the tank to career over the edge, fortunately without any injuries to the shaken crew.

(Above) Callsign 'Three Zero', the troop leader's Challenger of 3rd Tp, C Sqn, QRH, on the Glamoc ranges; the green flag denotes that its weapons are unloaded and the laser is switched off. The ranges were about two hours' distance from C Sqn's camp at Bosanski Petrovac, from where one tank from each troop was rotated through the range for one day at a time. This maintained the crews' gunnery skills, including the long range HESH techniques which would be desirable should general hostilities occur in Bosnia. Each crew fired about 12 main armament rounds, half HESH and half DST, and some 1,000 rounds through the coax and commander's machine guns.

This tank has a confusingly mixed set of markings due to inter-squadron attachments and the handing over of MBTs to replacement elements. The black triangle on the turret side and forward bazooka plate indicates A Sqn, and has not been changed to a circle when the tank was taken over by C Squadron. Meanwhile, the black pig painted on the top face of the TOGS barbette is the unmistakable sign of the D Sqn troop attached to C Sqn, though the black rectangle on its side lacks the usual white New Zealand fern.

(Opposite top) HEREFORD, the Challenger 1 Mk 3 Control Tank of the Command Troop, HQ Sqn, 1st The Queen's Dragoon Guards disembarks from the Ukrainian vessel *Yuryi Maskarov* on 20 June 1996. Flying the regimental standard of the Hapsburg eagle and the Red Dragon national flag of Wales, Major Patrick Andrews' 'Two Two Bravo' was the first vehicle ashore, marking the arrival of the 'Welsh Cavalry' in suitable style. As usual disembarkation had to wait until the world's news media were ready to record the event. The other Challenger in the Command Troop belongs to the CO, Lt Col Hamish Macdonald, whose tank 'One One Bravo' is named HARLECH. The vehicles of the HQ Sqn have names beginning with H, whereas the sabre squadrons carry place names in Wales beginning with their corresponding letter.

For the next four days, Scammell Commander tank transporters ferried the Challengers of the QDG Battlegroup into Bosnia on a 24-hour round trip, carrying those of the QRH back on the return leg. The QDG assumed command from the QRH at 1200hrs on 24 June. C Squadron were attached to 2nd Canadian Bde. and D Sqn to 1 (UK) Mech.Bde. within IFOR's Multi-National Division (South-West).

(Right) CAERPHILLY, a Mark 3 of 3rd Tp, C Sqn, QDG commanded by Sgt Caulfield, conducts a patrol in the area around Bosanski Petrovac where C Sqn were based. The patrol pro-gramme was based on a three-day cycle with a day of maintenance, and was designed to reassure the local population of the powerful and impartial presence of IFOR - while convincing the FWF that an imperfect peace was preferable to a return to hostilities and confrontation with IFOR air and ground forces.

The Challengers of the QDG Battlegroup were painted in plain forest green rather than standard British Army camouflage of black stripes over a green base; the number of white rings on the fume extractor indicates the troop within the squadron. Note the later style 'bubble gum' warning light at the rear of the turret. The tank also carries the standard markings applied to British Army vehicles during Operation Resolute: the IFOR legend in white capitals, and the inverted black chevron echoing that displayed by Coalition Forces during the Gulf War.

(Opposite top) Lt Dominic Roberts supervises maintenance on his Mark 3, ST DAVIDS, during a halt near Baraci, a small hill village in the middle of 'The Anvil' where D Sqn, QDG were based. A rotating programme saw each sabre troop spend one week at Baraci undertaking guard duties, maintenance and some local patrolling; one week at the 'Red Dragon' checkpoint at Straichi; another week at Baraci doing Quick Reaction Force patrols throughout the expanding area of operations using MBTs, Scimitars, Land Rovers, mountain bikes, helicopters and, of course, feet; and finally one week at 'Cold Hussar'. D Squadron was attached to 1st Bn, The Worcestershire & Sherwood Foresters Regiment, providing the essential armour mix of MBTs and Warriors in the Woofers' battlegroup. The coloured spot on the TOGS barbette is the regimental insignia. (Walter Böhm)

(Left) During the first few months of Operation Resolute 2A, the Challengers of 1st The Queen's Dragoon Guards covered high mileages as they came to dominate their AOR in the lead-up to important popular elections on September 14. Eventually the Battlegroup operational area extended to some 10,000sq/km, with the attendant problems of supplying far-flung units. Here, a diminutive civilian Fiat follows warily behind HARLECH, the tank of the CO, Lt Col Hamish Macdonald, during a road patrol between Bosanski Petrovac and Kljuc. The Challengers of the Command Troop were often combined with a pair of Scimitars to form an extra sabre troop for increased operational flexibility, while the CO covered his extensive AOR in Land Rover and Gazelle helicopter. Flying the Union Flag from one of its three radio antennae, 78KF92 has the TOGS barbette door emblazoned with the Red Dragon of Wales.

(Above & inset) Summer 1996; a pair of Challengers of 3rd Tp, C Sqn, QDG stand guard at the IEBL checkpoint 'White Fang' on the main route between Sanski Most (a Bosnian Muslim town) and Prijedor (a Bosnian Serb town). 'White Fang', named after a particularly vicious local dog, was near the village of Koprivna on the west bank of the River Sana; following the September elections a full troop was stationed there for three weeks to control movement of ethnic groups through the ZOS between Sanski Most and Prijedor. These Challengers have their main armament fitted with plastic muzzle covers and no longer carry the commander's L37A2 machine gun. It is the nature of peacekeeping operations that such incongruous sights abound: a £1 million-plus MBT deployed far overseas to protect elderly peasants and their haycart.

(Opposite top) During Resolute 2A, QDG LAD Main was colocated with C Sqn at Bosanski Petrovac, along with the remainder of the Echelon. Besides their essential recovery and repair tasks the LAD were widely employed for G5 projects to help rebuild the local infrastructure, ranging from the repair of ambulances and fire engines to refurbishing whole schools and their playgrounds using the CRARRV dozer blade. Here, the C Sqn CRARRV negotiates Tank Bridges laid by Chieftain AVLB of the Royal Engineers alongside a Medium Girder Bridge on the road from Sanski Most to Prijedor.

On deployment to Bosnia each of the two QDG sabre squadrons was equipped with an extra six CVR(T) Scimitars and nine extra wheeled vehicles, but with no increase in manpower (these Scimitars were in addition to those of the Reconnaissance Troop). Accordingly, crewmen had to be cross-trained on CVR(T) and Challenger.

(Left) Challengers of D Sqn, QDG fire on the move against targets on the Glamoc ranges on 20 August 1996, as the crews hone their operational skills prior to the potentially troublesome elections in early September. The range was also known as Range Resolute Barbara - Resolute after the operational name, and Barbara after the patron saint of the Royal Artillery, who first set up the range on a former Serbian Army training area. The targets for the tanks were car wrecks doused with old sump oil and petrol to give a satisfying explosion. (Given the local standard of driving in Bosnia there is always a plentiful supply of such wrecks.) Note that the auxiliary fuel drums of QDG Challengers were commonly used for their intended purpose to extend road ranges, rather than as crew stowage containers; and that D Sqn painted the lids of the turret rear stowage bins orange as an air recognition feature.

It is worthy of note that B Sqn of 1st The Queen's Dragoon Guards also deployed to Bosnia in 1996, but as mechanized infantry in Saxon APCs with 1st Bn, The Royal Green Jackets - such is the versatility of the Royal Armoured Corps as it enters the new millennium, when the QDG convert once more from MBTs to the armoured reconnaissance role.

(Above) On 6 December 1996 The Royal Scots Dragoon Guards (Carabiniers & Greys) assumed control from the QDG as the tank element of Operation Resolute 3A. They soon imposed their identity as the 'Scottish Cavalry' - shown to dramatic effect by this Challenger 1 Mk 3 of the Command Troop, HQ Sqn, flying the cross of St Andrew and a large regimental flag during a patrol through the village of Belajce near Mrkonjic Grad. The two Challengers of the Command Troop commonly acted independently as part of Battlegroup HQ and were often employed on 'hearts and minds' tasks throughout the AOR - even dispensing magazines and other small luxuries to the dislocated populace. 'One One Bravo', the CO's tank, is traditionally emblazoned in the SCOTS DG with the Scottish Lion; it soon became known as 'The Lion of Belajce', and in the absence of the CO was commanded by the Drum Major. 'Two Two Bravo', the Second-in-Command's tank, is shown here with Sgt Burns as commander and L/Cpl Thomson as loader; they wear the regimental grey beret recalling the old Royal Scots Greys.

(Opposite) After its lamentable early reputation for unreliability, Challenger 1 has proved to be highly successful in Bosnia in terms of both availability and reliability, which have risen dramatically the more the tanks have been used as compared to the normal tempo in Germany. During good weather the tanks were averaging approximately 100km a week, though considerably less during snow or icy conditions when it often became too hazardous to deploy the MBTs on operations except in a dire emergency. However, this presupposes the dedicated attention of both the crews and the REME Light Aid Detachment.

Here Sgt Edwards and Cpl Joyce of the REME Fitters Section prepare to remove a powerpack at the SCOTS DG LAD Main workshops at the bus depot near Mrkonjic Grad in January 1997; note in the background the 7th Armoured Brigade 'desert rat' on the TOGS door, and below it the St Andrew's cross sticker (which seems to break out like a noble rash wherever Scottish soldiers have access to a few square inches of flat steel). The skills and dedication of the Royal Electrical & Mechanical

Engineers are fundamental to all operations conducted by the British Army, and the more successful they are the less they are noticed.

(Above) The Royal Scots Dragoon Guards deployed to Bosnia with three composite squadrons comprising personnel drawn from throughout the regiment, and these temporary squadrons were named after regimental battle honours. Thus HQ Sqn was known as Salerno Squadron, while the two others were Waterloo (after perhaps the most famous battle of the old Royal Scots Greys), and Nunshigum Squadron (after a famous action fought by the old 3rd Carabiniers in Burma during the Second World War). Waterloo Sqn was the reconnaissance element, with 16 CVR(T) Scimitars, and Nunshigum Sqn had 12 Challengers - although it was standard practice to combine AFVs from both for increased flexibility. Depending on the situation a typical patrol comprised two Scimitars and one Challenger, with a Land Rover carrying the patrol commander and an interpreter.

Exactly one year after the Dayton peace accord was signed, IFOR was reduced in scale and became SFOR or Stabilisation Force. SFOR was configured for 'peace management' rather than 'peace implementation' – that is, it was assumed that the local factions actually wanted peace, rather than having to be persuaded of its advantages – although the practical role remained much the same. In the British Army, the change of mandate brought a new operational codename; Operation Resolute became Operation Lodestar, and the IFOR markings were altered to SFOR (however, in the SCOTS DG area of operations the local populace were taught that SFOR stood for 'Scottish Force'). Here, a CRARRV of Nunshigum Sqn is driven off a Scammell Commander at Gornji Vakuf during February 1997, giving a forceful impression as to why this powerful vehicle is now known as Rhino.

(**Opposite**) In the next roulement (rotation of units) the SCOTS DG were replaced by The King's Royal Hussars on 6 June 1997.

The mountainous terrain and primitive roads of much of Bosnia have proved to be a serious impediment to the mobility of MBTs and indeed many heavy trucks, which has caused major resupply problems for remote hilltop positions such as OPs (observation posts) and communications Rebro (rebroadcast) stations. Accordingly, given their affinity for horses, the British cavalry regiments deployed to Bosnia have acquired local animals, some fitted with stores panniers for supplying outposts, to conduct operational patrols over difficult mountain tracks. Perhaps predictably, such horse-mounted patrols caused wide interest in the British press - whereas the solid if less photogenic success of IFOR/SFOR

had effectively reduced media interest in the affairs of the former Republic of Yugoslavia to almost nil.

It is not difficult to see in this photograph the dangers inherent to MBTs on narrow mountain tracks, where the crumbling roadside is liable to collapse under the weight of a 70 tonne Challenger and send it crashing down the hillside.

Owned by local Bosnian Serb farmers, the horses each cost 20 Deutsche Marks (approximately £8) per day to hire. Such patrols were conducted once or twice a week by the KRH, who also reintroduced another venerable form of transport into Bosnia - a regimental hot air balloon, used for G5 operations to entrance local children and entertain notables.

(**Above**) Although the purely military aspects of SFOR operations have much diminished during Operation Lodestar, and civil affairs now predominate, British forces periodically show their teeth during demonstrations at the Glamoc ranges. In concert with the other five nations of MND(SW), up to 21 different weapon systems are co-ordinated in a symphony of overwhelming firepower to impress local warlords of the FWF. These need to be reminded repeatedly that breaking the peace would not be in their best interests, and that SFOR troops have the speed of response and operational capability to reach any point in the divisional area with a force which the FWF's Soviet-derived weapon systems could never hope to match.

Like the previous cavalry regiments, The King's Royal Hussars deployed sabre squadrons with 12 Challengers

and six CVR(T) Scimitars to increase operational flexibility, as shown here by C Sqn, KRH at the conclusion of a firepower demonstration - with an American AH-64 Apache attack helicopter hovering overhead. Note the KRH regimental insignia on the TOGS barbette doors of the Challengers and on the thermal imaging cowlings of the SPIRE-fitted Scimitars. The KRH wear brown berets with crimson badge backing, reminiscent of the special regimental headgear of the old 11th Hussars during the Second World War.

Since these pictures were taken other cavalry regiments have been deployed in the tank and armoured recce role, and the British Army commitment to Bosnia continues.

(Above) Challenger was only ever intended as an interim measure before a definitive design was to supersede Chieftain. Despite huge expenditure on abortive joint and unilateral development programmes during the 1970s-80s, no tank emerged to fit the operational requirements of the British Army. Accordingly Vickers Defence Systems offered a private venture design based on the hull and automotives of Challenger, and a modified turret of their current export model MBT incorporating the latest fire control technology, derived from that which had proved so successful for the M1 and M1A1 Abrams during the Canadian Army Trophy NATO gunnery competition in 1987. Originally designated Challenger 2 Mark 2, the new model was finally called Challenger 2 for

simplicity and all previous Challengers were redesignated Challenger 1. In January 1987, Vickers Defence Systems were awarded a contract to build nine of these prototype Challenger 2 MBTs. (VDS)

(Opposite top) With the introduction of new procurement procedures allowing competitive tendering from foreign countries, Challenger 2 was pitted against rivals from the USA (M1A2), Germany (Leopard 2 Improved) and France (Leclerc). After extensive trials in which each model excelled in one aspect or another, Challenger 2 was chosen as the successor to Chieftain; but only 127, together with 13 Driver Training Tanks, were to be acquired to serve alongside the existing Challenger 1 fleet. Here, prototype V9 fires its L30

high pressure main armament on the Royal Armoured Corps ranges at Lulworth. Despite the use of three-piece ammunition, an experienced crew has achieved a rate of fire of eight rounds in 42 seconds, all of which hit their targets.

(Right) Following the success of Challenger 1 during the Gulf War, its successor was offered to several Middle Eastern countries as they rearmed in the face of the continuing threat posed by the Iraqi regime. While Kuwait had been equipped with Chieftain prior to the Iraqi invasion, it felt no need to replace them with any further British MBTs and purchased Abrams M1A2s instead (although the Kuwaiti Army decided to procure Warrior IFVs in preference to Bradley).

Here, a prototype model of

Challenger 2 is shown during demonstration trials in Saudi Arabia following the Gulf War - below the registration plate 06SP95 is the Arabic inscription 'Desert Defender'. This vehicle has an exterior thermal insulation layer on the turret and hull front which reduces the internal temperature by 8°C as compared to external ambient temperature, although the tank also has a highly efficient air conditioning system to control the internal atmosphere. In its first overseas sales, Challenger 2 has been purchased by Oman in a contract for 18 MBTs, two Driver Training Tanks, four CRARRVs, nine UNIPOWER tank transporters and four Alvis Stormer command post vehicles. (Dennis Lunt)

Challenger 2 was accepted for service with the British Army on 25 July 1994, but continuing acceptance trials at ATDU Bovington revealed a number of faults in the turret systems which delayed the in-service date until they were fully resolved. These problems did not prevent the British Army from ordering a further 259 Challenger 2 MBTs in the following year, with the intention to replace all Chieftain and Challenger 1 MBTs with a single-type fleet of 386 Challenger 2s.

Despite a superficial visual similarity between Challenger 1 and 2, there is in fact only a 3 per cent commonality between the two; so it is all the more surprising that the new MBT was not given a new name to increase export prospects, given the fact that Challenger 1 never achieved any overseas sales. Among the many improvements over Challenger 1, Challenger 2 has a David Brown TN54 transmission with six forward and two reverse

gears; a second generation Hydrogas variable spring rate suspension system, with double pin tracks whose tension can be hydraulically adjusted remotely from the driver's seat (previously this task had to be undertaken manually by the crew with a gigantic spanner).

(Opposite top) Although mobility and reliability have been much improved, the greatest advances have been made to the fighting aspects or 'fightability' of Challenger 2. Firepower has been enhanced by the installation of a high pressure L30 120mm rifled gun and a new range of CHARM 3 ammunition, coupled to a fully integrated 'Hunter-Killer' fire control system with a stabilized panoramic commander's day sight and stabilized gunner's sight. These incorporate a second generation TOGS thermal imaging system, with the sight picture available to both the commander and gunner on relaxed view monitors, or else

injected into the gunner's primary sight. The TOGS housing is now mounted above the main armament for better alignment. This Challenger 2 took part in Operation Cray on 18 September 1996 - a demonstration before the overseas delegates of the Joint Arms Control Implementation Group - during which it successfully engaged six targets in 26 seconds.

(Right) Overcoming the principal deficiencies of its predecessor, Challenger 2 has a sophisticated fire control system incorporating a comprehensive array of sighting devices. The commander's primary sight is a gyroscopically stabilized panoramic sight, capable of 360° independent traverse, with an integral Neodymium Yag laser rangefinder, and the capability of aligning the main armament to his line of sight at any time. The gunner can observe independently and engage targets in either the visual or thermal modes, the latter by

means of TOGS, which can be seen in the gunner's primary sight as well as in relaxed view monitors for the gunner and commander.

The combination of the primary sights allows the gunner to observe the primary arc while the commander maintains all-round observation. If the latter sees a target which he considers to be a greater threat than that being observed by the gunner, he can lase the target and immediately align the gun onto it. As the gunner engages this priority target, the commander is already searching for or lasing a new target. This technique is known as 'Hunter-Killer', and forms the basis of most modern MBT fire control systems.

Challenger 2 is now in service with the British Army in Germany, and by the end of the year 2000 it will equip six armoured regiments.

63

The latest vehicle in the range is Challenger 2E, specifically designed to function effectively in hot climates and desert regions. Challenger 2E combines British advanced armour technology with a German powertrain, French sighting devices and a North American fire control system to create an MBT with outstanding armour protection, firepower and mobility. The latter is provided by a 1,500bhp V-12 MTU 883 transversely mounted turbocharged engine, coupled to a RENK HSWL 295 automatic transmission with five forward and three reverse gears, giving a power-to-weight ratio of 24bhp per tonne in temperatures up to 55°C. During a trial conducted for the Saudi Arabian National Guards in 1997 a Desert Challenger (as the 2E was then called) covered 3,377km without one major failure. As part of the trial a powerpack exchange was undertaken using a CRARRV; the entire procedure took 36 minutes, from the moment the tank stopped to the moment it moved off again under its own power.

With a top speed of 80kph and a sustained road speed of 72kph, and road/cross-country ranges of 550 and 250km, the 2E has remarkable agility for a tank weighing over 60 tonnes. In place of a cupola-mounted GPMG, the loader is provided with a .50 cal. Browning MG for area defence. The fire control system has been yet further enhanced, with a commander's panoramic thermal imager, and an integrated battlefield management system incorporating a tactical display unit with digital inputs from a GPS navigation system, information from other vehicles within the unit, and real-time secure communications with higher formations. The driver has a thermal imaging night driving viewer, the aperture of which is visible here in the glacis plate above the centre of the registration number. Unlike all previous British tanks, the driver steers using a wheel rather than tillers; he also has a powerpack information display unit to monitor its performance and warn him of any problems. (VDS; & The Tank Museum)